The author was born in 1945 in a small town called Belvedere which lies between Dartford in Kent, and Woolwich in London. He went to a small primary school and was taught by Catholic nuns. He is a Catholic himself and his religion is very important to him. He failed his 11+ exams and went on to attend a Church of England secondary school.

He left school at fifteen and started an engineering apprenticeship, he had a natural aptitude for the job.

For Mrs Wendy Clarke, the manager of the Care Home
I'm living in. She is an inspiration.

Kevin Patrick Harry O'Connor

AN APPRENTICE'S LIFE

AUSTIN MACAULEY PUBLISHERS™

LONDON · CAMBRIDGE · NEW YORK · SHARJAH

A CIP catalogue record for this title is available from the British Library.

ISBN 9781398458598 (Paperback)
ISBN 9781398458604 (ePub e-book)

www.austinmacauley.com

First Published 2022
Austin Macauley Publishers Ltd®
1 Canada Square
Canary Wharf
London
E14 5AA

Thank you to Mrs Wendy Clarke, and half a dozen of the staff who urged me to get my manuscript published.

With Love from

Kevin O'Connor,
The Roving Vagabond,
to Max.

Interview in the "Arsenal"

In April 1960, I had to go for an interview at the Royal Ordnance Factory, Woolwich, R.O.F (W). I was sent, through the post, a very important letter which, when I opened it, was from the Ministry of Defence War Department, telling me to attend an interview for an engineering apprenticeship in the "arsenal". The letter included the time and date of the interview along with a small sheet of paper authorising me entry to this august factory.

The day finally came and I marched off down the garden path with my train fare and sheet of paper, so that I could get in through the main gate on Beresford Square in Woolwich. I got on the train and was whisked from Belvedere Railway station, passing through Abbey Wood station, Plumstead station, and alighting at Woolwich Arsenal station. I had a walk of about 100 yards from the station to the main gate where I had to show my piece of paper to the Ministry of Defence Policeman on the "gate". He scrutinised my piece of paper and waved me in. There was a passageway in the main gate for pedestrians and a wide passage big enough for Tank Transporters and all manner of vehicles, from "top brass" to motorised workmen and women. At each side of the wide entrance were two 16" Battleship gun shells buried in the road protecting the bridleway of the main gate. They were buried in the road about 18 inches deep with the point of the shells upwards and standing about 18 inches above the ground. The main gate had windows above the passageway and the building was dated 1726 if I remember rightly. There were two more shells buried in the ground on the inside of the gate to protect the corners of the building from traffic leaving the factory. I found the building where my interview was to be held, passing the Arsenal's own fire brigade – half a dozen fire engines parked under cover, and then the ambulances, and doctors and nurse's quarters. I went inside and was told by an elderly gent with a Sergeant Major's moustache to sit down outside this door, which was where the interview was to be conducted. The time finally came for my interview and I was ushered in by the "Sergeant Major" who then closed the door behind me. I was confronted by four men sitting on the other side of a large polished brown wooden table, all looking at me. In front of me was a wooden chair facing them where I was told to sit down. The interview began. One man was taking notes, and the other three began to cross-examine me asking a number of questions, one of which was what hobby or hobbies did I have. I told them that I liked making aircraft from Balsa wood, tissue paper and "dope". I almost saw their ears prick up, and one of them asked me, what is meant by "DIHEDRAL".

I told him that, looking at the side elevation of the aircraft, the DIHEDRAL was where the wings were canted up at an angle, leading edge up, so that the passing air would give the aeroplane lift while it was flying through the air. At last, the interview was over and I was given leave to go.

I was red-faced and sweating and felt a huge feeling of relief. I had to show another piece of paper giving me permission to leave, and then I was out on Beresford Square again! This square was where an open market was held every day of the week except Sundays. I loved hearing the street vendors bawling out their wares; "Apples a pound, pears, they're lovely". "'Ere you are Mrs. A lovely cauliflower. To you Madam – 6d" (Six pence in old money).

Sixpence was more commonly known as a "tanner". There was also the:

- Thrupenny bit – 3 old pennies.
- "3a-pence" – 1 ½ old pennies,
- Ha'penny – ½ an old penny
- Farthing – ¼ old penny
- Penny Farthing – 1 ¼ old pennies
- Penny 3 Farthings – 1 ¾ old pennies
- Shilling – 12 old pennies
- Florin – 2 shillings
- 2 shillings and sixpence/half a crown/half a dollar (There was about 4 dollars to the pound then)
- Ten-shilling note
- One pound note
- Five-pound note
- Ten-pound note
- Twenty-pound note
- And so on…

There was 20 shillings to the pound, 240 old pennies to the pound, and that's about it. My old Grandad said to me that evening when he came home from work (B.I.C.C. – British Insulated Callendar's Cables), Crabtree Manorway, Belvedere, about ½ a mile from where I and my brothers and sisters were born, "How did you do it Kev, you went off with such confidence, I could never have done that". I said, "I don't know Grandad - I just did!" I got a letter a few weeks later from the Ministry of Defence War Department, telling me that I had been accepted as an apprentice in the Woolwich Arsenal. And that, in due course my indentures would be sent for myself, my Dad, and Grandad to sign. The letter also mentioned that I would start my apprenticeship on August 29th, 1960, ending on June 30th, 1966.

*****

My old Nan as a proper comedienne. She would say "She was so ugly – she had a face like a busted boot", or "She had a face like the back of a bus".

When we were about eight or nine years old, she would hold her fist up in front of your face with her arm crooked up and t hen say, as she pushed her fist out to flatten your nose "SMELL IT!" Before she pushed her fist out, with her arm still crooked, she'd say, "SEE THAT?!" and then "SMELL IT!" (I made a mess of that joke, didn't I?)

Around about (I'm jumping ahead a bit) 1962, I used to cycle up to Plumstead (a distance of about 4 miles) to a small street market, and buy a pint of brown shrimps, put them in a shopping bag, hang the bag on the handlebars and cycled back home, where I would sit next to my Grandad at the tea table on a Saturday afternoon, and between the two of us, we would, with bread and butter and a mug of tea each, scoff the lot. This always took place on a Saturday afternoon in the summertime. My Grandad introduced me to brown shrimps – they had to be brown. I loved them – and him, equally. He was a dear man. He didn't fight in the first World War as he had flat feet. He was born in 1892 and my Nan in 1894. They both lived to be 86. I will always remember when my Grandad died, my Nan said to my Mum "I don't want to go on without him V." (V was short for Vera, my mum), but she got over it. She was tough, but her heart was in the right place. My Nan always said, when talking about the Second World War, that my Dad's indomitable spirit got them through the War.

My dad wanted to join the Royal Navy but was turned down as he was in a reserved occupation (a millwright – maintenance fitter) in the Arsenal. My Grandad was an electrician in the Arsenal at the time. He was taken on as an electrician's mate but soon proved to be good enough to be "Made up" to full electrician, with a mate of his own/ My Grandad, like my Dad, was highly intelligent. They both worked all over the Arsenal and when big guns were being tested down the "Abbey Wood End" as that area was known, in the proof butts, men who work working up ladders were told to come down, anything up to a mile from where the gun was about to be tested, as the blast would (and has) blown men off their ladders causing serious injury if they were unlucky or killed. My Nan was working in the Arsenal between the Wars filling Battle-ship Gun (16") shells with cordite – highly dangerous. The women had to remove anything made of metal from underneath themselves, like bracelets, watches, rings, etc., because of the danger of these articles causing sparks which would cause an almighty detonation, killing all the women in the special concrete blockhouses called "Danger Buildings" which had walls and roofs, two foot think solid concrete with earthen banking built up all around the Danger Building up to just above roof height with a 20ft moat around the whole lot of it. The earthen banking caused any accidental blast to go upwards, and the moat stopped fire spreading. The women had to strip naked and don a special overall, remove their shoes, and don wooden clogs.

Some of the women used to chew pieces of cordite to get a "high" but it rotted their teeth! The moats were twenty feet wide and encircled the whole lot.

*****

Beresford Square. "Ours is a nice house, ours is, it's got no rats nor mouses." I just had to get that one off my chest! I digress. Beresford Square is about 70 yards square, made of granite bricks laid down flat and level, and at that time was criss-crossed with tramlines, the last of which, ran in 1952. My dad took me and my brother, Tony, on one of the last trams out of Woolwich, home to Belvedere, and we still have the tickets somewhere. To the left of the main gate, a narrow road ran down towards the River Thames alongside the ten-foot-high wall which kept the Arsenal secure from interlopers and was known as Rope Yard Rails for obvious reasons and was where the barrow boys used to park their stout barrows for the night, pulling them up to the market early in the mornings, laden with fresh produce. The barrows had two shafts by which the barrow boys dragged them.

They had small wooden cart-wheels just like a horse drawn cart only smaller. The market had been there for one hundred years or more. Nearby, down on the river, the Woolwich Free Ferry ran from morning to night carrying everything from big heavy lorries right down to bicycles. One of the ferries was called, or rather, named, Ernest Bevin, a Politician. There were three of these ferries, two of them running to and fro across the river, passing each other midstream, the Captains were experts at their craft. The ferries had steam engines, two of them, with paddle wheels half way along their hulls. By running one engine full ahead, and the other full astern, they could turn through 180° while not moving up or down river.

They had two funnels painted black with fancy tops, and the public could go down one deck and see the steam engines working through the windows which afforded a fascinating sight to anyone who was interested. These huge connecting rods with enormous Big-End bearings driving the shafts round and round, turning the paddle wheels. Every part of those engines was kept shining brightly, everything highly polished by the makers. Occasionally you might be lucky and see an engineer in his white boiler suit checking oil levels/ The big-end bearings were lubricated by a rectangular steel box which had to be kept full of oil with two wicks emerging from the boxes of oil and dangling down, where every time the big-end bearing came up and over and round and round it would just brush against these oil-soaked "wicks" taking oil with it. The boxes full of oil were suspended at exactly the right position to enable this to happen. The engineer has to replenish the box with lubricating oil at regular intervals, making sure it never ran dry.

The two funnels were either side of the ferry, not in line ahead but abreast, and half way along the ferry above the boiler room and hand fed furnaces. At another window you could see the stokers shovelling coal into the furnaces. Floating pontoon jetties both sides of the river took the traffic on and off the ferries allowing for the ever-changing level of the river's tides.

The captain had to line up the ferries exactly in the right place so that the pontoons could take the traffic on and off. It was all clever stuff. The ferries had to be secured by stout ropes while this operation was carried out. My dad used to take us up to Woolwich to have rides back and forth on the ferries. One weekend we were spotted going back and forth and my dad was told to take me and Tony off the ferry as this wasn't allowed. The third ferry was being overhauled. There was always one ferry being overhauled and on standby until one of the working ferries needed an overhaul. There was a tunnel under the Thames within 30 yards of the ferries for pedestrians to walk across to the far bank of the river. The tunnels were dug by hand under the mud and silt etc, through firm earth and lined inside with shining white tiles. They were circular inside with a flat concrete walkway, and you could hear echoing voices right up the other end of the tunnel.

There were identical lifts either side of the river on the banks carrying people and bicycles down to the level of the tunnel. There was also a spiral staircase for people who didn't want to wait for the lift. The spiral staircase ran round and round the lift shaft. I will always remember the sense of loss I felt when I was five or six years old, playing with a lead bodied small toy lorry about two inches long on the ferry. My dad was holding onto me while I pushed the toy lorry backwards and forwards and it fell down into the river and was gone forever. With it being lead, it will probably still be down there somewhere to this day, seventy years on. Makes you think, doesn't it!? The ferries connected the North and South Circular roads, the A206

*****

August 29th, 1960

My apprenticeship begins. My mum had made me some sandwiches for tea break, my dad got me up at 6.45am as I had to be in to work at 8am. He made me a slice of toast and a cup of tea, I got dressed and came down to the "kitchen" (our dining room) – the kitchen proper was known as the scullery – and ate my toast and drank my tea, my dad having already left for work as he had an earlier start than me. I had a quarter mile walk to Belvedere station where I caught the train. It took nine minutes to get to Woolwich Arsenal railway station, leaving me a ¼ mile walk in through the main gate and then straight ahead past the fire engines and ambulances to building A75, the Apprentice Training Shop. I had been sent my gate pass through the post a week earlier, which I had to show the M.O.D. Police on the gate. As I approached the Training Shop, my stomach full of butterflies, I passed a line of parked cars, one of which caught my eye. It was a vintage sports car with outside exhausts, painted royal blue, and in white, along the side of the bonnet, both sides, were the words "BACCHANALIAN CHARIOT".

There were two big double doors made of wood and they were shut but there was a small door to get into the building A75 fitted into the larger door. You had to step over a "step" about nine inches high and pass through the small door at the same time. Inside the workshop, which was about 40 yards square, were dozens of machines and a fitter's bench running straight along the right-hand side of the building, with two steam pipes near ground level for heating. On the far side of the building were large windows, with more fitter's benches.

These were jutting out from the wall at right angles, big enough for two boys to work at. All the boys had a six-inch vice and an electric light on a flexible length of steel levers about four feet long in all. I followed some boys into our locker room and found an empty locker where I took off my jacket and hung it on a hook in the locker. I left my sandwiches on a shelf about a foot from the top of the locker, which was about six feet high. My dad had bought "bib-and-brace" overalls which were blue in colour and were the right size for me. Someone gave me a piece of thick paper with my name on it which fitted into the outside of the door, and in the lock was a key. I locked the locker door and we were told to follow this fine man of 6'3" into a classroom adjacent to the workshop. The man was Mr. Alec Stevens, Mr Stevens to us. He told us to sit down at the desks. He was about fifty-five years old, straight-backed, and wore a white coat which was an overall with two or three pens and pencils in the breast pocket. He had blue eyes, large black pupils, a rugged "broken" nose, and a blue jowl, he needed to shave twice a day. He had dark blue pin-striped trousers and good quality polished black shoes on. He introduced himself in a deep, gravelly voice and got on with the lesson. On the wall behind him was an oil cloth, accurate depiction of a 0 to 1 micrometre with the "works" exposed for us all to study. The oil cloth was about 4 feet wide by about 3 feet deep. After explaining what this measuring instrument was for, and its parts, he asked us boys what the reading on the micrometre was. I did some quick calculations in my mind, and hoping I'd got it right, I put my hand up. I was the quickest boy in the class YES – I was right. He was well pleased with me, at 5 feet 1 inches tall, the shortest boy in the class of 40 boys. GOD was I pleased and proud of myself, little Kevin, the quickest off the mark. Mr. Stevens said, "well done lad", and gave me a smile. I was walking on air! Mr Stevens was it turned out assistant foreman and turning instructor. I forgot to mention; Mr Stevens had a white collar and tie. I was put working with Peter Happy, who was tall and broad and permanently tanned and bespectacled.

I was right on the end of the bench nearest to the double wooden doors which were opened wide on hot days and had windows in the top half of them, where green leaved trees could be seen – a lovely antidote to all that hard metal and concrete floors. Our fitting instructors name was Mr. Jack Connors, bald except for the sides and back and a little overweight at 5 feet 4 inches tall. He was from the north of England and had a broad north-country accent and wore spectacles which always found their way down to the end of his nose! We started off making large and small outside calipers and large and small inside calipers – our first job. We were issued with proper draughtsman drawings of these calipers and set to work, and it was hard work. First of all, we cut out of steel plate, the rough shape of the calipers, then we filed them down to size and shape, exactly as per drawing, then we had to file them down to exactly the right thickness and were allowed a tolerance of plus or minus .005 or 5 thousandths.

Dinner-time or lunch-time if you're posh came round and we all sprinted down to the Flagstaff canteen, which had two separate eating halls. Downstairs was for men in overalls and upstairs was for cleanly attired people, nearly all of them office workers. We went upstairs! We had been issued food vouchers so our dinner, or lunch, didn't cost us a penny. We had all been invited to join the R.O.F.S.A. (Royal Ordnance Factory Sports Association) so, on a full belly we ran a quarter of a mile up to this fairly old building of 6 floors, we ran up the stairs to the top floor, where there were, to my amazement, three full size billiard tables, and one-half size table, all with full sets of snooker balls and billiard balls, and long queues (extra-long) long and short rests and "spider". This is where I learnt to play snooker Peter Happy turned out to be my best friend during my time in the arsenal, I always remember him saying with a laugh "I can't be anything else but happy with a name like mine". I can remember his address to this day – 21 Kimberly Drive, Albany Park, Sidcup, Kent. I wonder is he still with us? When it's my turn to go to heaven, we will meet again. R.I.P.

Peter was a motorcycle fan. He had a Royal Enfield Crusader Sports, a 250, his first bike all electric red and chrome. Royal Enfield's motto is "made like a gun". I remember one worker, a labourer, who jokingly said "If they're made like a gun then they're the last bike I'd buy!" The afternoon passed, 5 o'clock came and we all knocked off, washed our hands with "Swarfega" which gets oil and grease off, very good stuff, and we got our gear on and all went our separate ways. Quite a few of the boys had motorcycles, and I remember one chap of about 16 kicking away at the kickstart of what turned out to be a Velocette Venom Sports. More of that anon (Velocette's turned out to be my favourite marque). (I forgot to mention that we had to mark out the calipers before cutting and filing them to size with copper sulphate which is painted on the sheet of steel plate green and dried a beautiful copper colour. Then we marked out the shape of the calipers, the scribed lines showing up a clear bright shining steel colour. Also, we had to drill a hole through one leg of the calipers the correct size for the domed nut and bolt to go through. On the other leg of the calipers we had to drill a hole the correct size and file it into a 'D' hole with a ¼ square file and ¼ rat tail file. Then we had to fit 3 or 4 thin steel shims between the legs of the calipers and tighten them together with the shims pressed between the 2 legs to enable them to move in and out to various sizes like scissors. We tightened them with our own double ended spanner which we had to make while making the calipers.)

When I got home about a quarter to six my Dad had come in on the previous train and had just finished his dinner. My Mum got my dinner out of the oven and, whilst eating, told them both about my day. I was full of it. I had eaten 2 dinners that day and everyday throughout my apprenticeship I did the same. Physical work and running to catch trains and running to play snooker gave one an appetite.

I had a kip in the armchair and then walked "up the top" where me and about half a dozen teenage boys and a few girls, one named Lily Barnard and another named Elvie Croney, both travellers, congregated underneath a lamp post at the entrance to Frank's Park, named after a local dignitary by the name of Frank Beadle, who bequeathed his estate to the public in perpetuity before he died. Frank's park as it is affectionately known must never be built on. There is a wooden bandstand in the middle of the park where, at that time, Brass Bands played on a Sunday evening, and we used to get bitten badly by gnats, which is now something of the past. This only happened in the summer-time.

I had a brief dalliance with Lily Barnard for a few months, nothing serious though, just snogging, and light petting, nothing more than that. Lil was a smasher, with long, wavy brown hair, dark brown eyes, and a permanent tan on her skin. Her father's name was Belcher Barnard, a traveller who had finally settled, down in a cul-de-sac off of Brook Street about ½ a mile from the O'Connor's residence, with a number of other travellers who had settled down in cheap and cheerful bungalows with Mr Barnard. He was almost as fat as he was tall (about my height) with enormous hairy brown hands. Elvie Croney was blonde and bubbly with a bouffant hair style full of natural curls. She was more attractive more for her personality than her looks, although she certainly wasn't ugly.

My Grandad saw Frank Beadle out in his pony and trap on numerous occasions around 1900 – 1910. Grandad was born in Belvedere which is Italian for "beautiful view", and from the River Thames bank looking back at Belvedere and Abbey Wood about a mile or two off, it is a beautiful view with woods called Lesnes wood, where there are beautiful ruins of an abbey called Lesnes Abbey and Bostall Woods, taking one's gaze almost as far as Plumstead.

Lesnes Abbey ruins have octagonal stones marking the foundations of the columns which held up the roof of the abbey and mark out the aisle which led up to the original stone altar which is all there today and will be for hundreds of years to come. The bases of the columns are octagonal and are just a few inches proud of the grass growing in the abbey where they once were. The walls of the abbey are all still there but only about a few inches to about a few feet proud of the surrounding grass. Nearby is a beautiful rose garden and a children's playground where I used to play as a kid.

My Mum and her friend Nina, a good-looking 25-year-old used to take us along there with the latest addition to our family in our lovely old-fashioned leaf sprung black pram lined out in cream. The head gardener of the rose garden is Mr. George Armstrong, a Scot and a very powerfully built man with a broken nose which he got while boxing in the army during the war. He never ever talked about his war, not even to his wife "Bubbles", He was a near neighbour of ours, and used to cycle to work about a mile and quarter each way. Abbey Wood is the name taken from the ruined abbey and the wood.

I wanted to be a fitter and turner, but had to choose, after a few months into my apprenticeship, one or the other. I chose turner. My next job, after the making of the calipers, was turning, under Mr. Stevens. I had to make 4 screw jacks from solid lumps of mild steel 2 ½ inches in diameter and 3 inches long, and a length of mild steel bar 2 feet long and 1 ¼ inches in diameter. I was to do all the turning on a nice HOLBROOK lathe. Mr. Stevens took me through the first one, step by step and then I made the other 3 on my own. They all came out with in .001" (1 thousandth of an inch) of each other, nigh on perfect. The thread in the bodies of the jacks was 5/8" x 14 T.P.I. (threads per inch). I had to screw cut the screws to suit. He showed me the "American method", which, in theory, should work out the best way, and in practice, really does! The threads came out beautiful, shining spirals with tiny little radii at the crest and the root of the thread, and flanks with no tears. Once again, he showed me how to make the first one and then the three others I did myself. I was shown how to do "knurling" which makes hundreds of little "pyramids" and turns a slippery piece of smooth turned steel very easy to grip and turn one way or the other. I was learning fast! I also had to do some taper turning and some radius cutting with a form tool. I was loving it! A thread of 5/8" diameter x 14 T.P.I. IS 5/8" B.S.F. (British standard fine), a standard size. The thread in the jack body was simply drilled out to the core or root, diameter of the thread and then tapped out 5/8 B.S.F to suit the screw. Another job done.

Then it was back to Jack Connors (whoops – Mr.!) to make tool-makers clamps. Let's have a rest and get in the park with "Prince" our beautiful dog for 14 years. His mother was a Golden Retriever, but nobody knows who the father was. He was jet black with a white chest, a white tip to his tail about 2 ½ "long, a white tip to his offside front paw, a white tip to his nearside rear paw and a white tip to his chin. He was fully grown at 18 months, but not fully "filled out". He used to hate motorcycles and would chase after them. He was the same with some cars, and birds! I once saw him chase a baby bird down a stony road in the park, leap up and take the bird clean out of the air. The bird hadn't the sense to fly upwards, just kept flying at almost 4 feet above the ground. He used to put his head down, close his eyes and crash through brambles chasing foxes as well. He was a hunter / killer, but with a loving, noble personality. I loved him. He came home one day, his tongue hanging out, as always, as the weather was warm, and we noticed that his tongue was torn from about 1 inch from the tip of his tongue right through and out at the side from the centre, that is. I had to take him up to Plumstead on the bus, a number 698, to the P.D.S.A. where the vet had a look and straight away said, "a fighter aye" I was hurt at this remark and, "He never starts fights, but he is a good fighter. Will it interfere with his lapping of water or tea, he likes tea." The vet assured me it wouldn't impede his drinking or eating one little but, so, very relieved, I left a donation and took him back home on the bus. More of him anon.

Back to the "grind". The Toolmakers clamps we had to make were made from Cast Steel, the same as files, and contained 1.1% carbon so they could be hardened and tempered, which is a fascinating and beautiful process, about which I will tell you more soon. We made the clamps out of cast steel and then went under the tutelage of Mr. Ernie Stavely to make the 3/8" B.S.F. clamping screws which were 6" long and made from mild steel. The threads had to be screw-cut on the lathe, and being so long and relatively spindly, extra care had to be taken when cutting the threads, because if you put too deep a cut on, they would bend and you had to start again from scratch. Mr. Staveley or Stavely favoured the English method of screw-cutting, which is hit and miss, compared to the American Method. I liked Mr. Stavely very much, he was a gentleman. I used the American method and they turned out perfect if I do say so myself. The clamps and screws had to be "blued" over a gas flame, after engraving our name on them. They looked beautiful. The clamps, before bluing had to be lightly polished with emery cloth strips, held along the length of a file, starting with fairly coarse, emery cloth and finishing with fine. We had been given 7 months to make our tools, and for every week that we went or took over 7 months, so many marks would be knocked off. (We were marked out of 100).

Bonfire night approaching, in the evenings, and at the weekends, we started building our bonfire. We started with the centre pole, a slender young tree trunk about 10 feet long set into the hard packed sand of what we called the sand pit, about 30 yards inside Frank's Park, where bonfires had been built for donkeys' years. Then we collected dry old wood and dead bushes from round about the park, and when the weekend came, we went and asked the men who were clearing the Seamen's home grounds of trees for redevelopment if we could have some of the tree trunks, 4-foot lengths which they had cut up with chainsaws for our bonfire. They were only too pleased to oblige, as they were just burning them on their huge bonfire anyway. My Dad had some large "cold" chisels about 15" long and I asked him could I borrow them to split these 15" diameter (approximately) logs in quarters for our bonfire. (The "cold" chisels are for cutting steel). He said "go ahead" so I went down to the bottom of our back garden to our shed, where I later kept my motorbike and I selected 2 of these large chisels. We split these logs in half using the chisels and a 7lb club hammer, and then in half again so that we split the logs into quarters. We had to carry the logs, before splitting them, about 30 yards to a suitable spot where a giant tree was growing out of the hillside and had a large root exposed, making an ideal "V" block on which we rested the logs where they would be kept still.

Whilst doing this, I was lucky not to lose the sight of my left eye. We had been told in work never to use a chisel with a mushroomed head. The chisel I was using was badly mushroomed from years of use where the head of the chisel was continually battered by hammers and had begun to spread outwards in the shape of a mushroom. I was bashing away at the head of the chisel in the process of splitting one of these logs when, suddenly a piece of jagged, razor sharp metal forming part of the mushroom head flew into the lid of my eye within 1/16" of my eye ball. It was agony, a sharp piercing pain. I stood up from bending, and every blink of my eye was agony. I thought "Dear God, what have I done". I walked home and showed my Dad. He didn't panic, quite the opposite, he managed to get hold of the piece of steel by the tip of his forefinger and thumb and teased it out. This little operation was absolutely excruciating but what a relief. I knew I was taking a chance with that old chisel but went ahead and that's what happened. There was hardly any blood.

I went to Mr. Ray O'Neill's house, nearby in Brigstock Road (we lived in Thornton Road) and asked him if I could use his grinding machine where I ground off all the mushrooming and went back up to the Seamen's home ground (where we weren't supposed to be!) and resumed operations. We quartered about 10 of these logs and then carried them over to the sandpit and stacked them on the bonfire. That bonfire was the best in living memory. When it was burning at its height you couldn't get within 15 feet of it, the heat was so intense. Sparks were shooting up into the night sky and a tree nearby had its dead but still hanging on leaves shrivelled up 50 feet up.

Several young Mum's came with their young children but stood well back. We had brought with us potatoes and butter which our Mums had given us. About 9 O'clock that night we rolled potatoes into the still burning embers and had a feast. I ate the lot, ash, and all (nature boy). We started the bonfire off with a gallon of petrol which I bought from the local Petrol Station in a gallon can. I stood on Alan O'Neill's shoulders and poured some down the centre pole and all around the bonfire, then we all took sheets of newspapers rolled up into torches and stood around in a circle. We lit one torch, then all got our torches of paper flaming and spread out round the bonfire. I shouted "Go" and we all lit our section of the bonfire. We had a wonderful evening and didn't go home 'til midnight, lying on the hard packed sand eating our baked potatoes and 'yakking'. It was a great night, one which I will never forget. We quietened down eventually and watched the embers burning and glowing, the occasional gust of wind fanning them back to life every so often. Wonderful. We just contemplated towards the end, boys smoking and all of us perfectly relaxed and very happy and content.

A Night to Remember

The next job we had to do was the scribing block. This tool was used on a 'blue' plate, to mark out by scribing lines dead level, on a block of steel, like a breech block. The blue plate was a heavy piece of steel of varying sizes, anything from 2 feet wide by almost 18'' deep, and about 6'' thick, with lifting handles to 8 feet wide by 6 feet deep, used for marking out Breech rings and the like. A beech ring weighed about 12 hundredweight. The 'blue' in blue plate was where engineers blue, made up from fine blue powder mixed with oil, was smeared thinly on the perfectly flat surface of the blue plate, where one could check one's work for flatness by rubbing the surface of the work (job) on the blue plate where any high spots would show up in blue, and then the high spots were scraped off and checked again on the blue plate for flatness. This process was repeated until the surface of the work showed up perfectly flat. The scribing block had a heavy base with a 'stick' of silver steel (high carbon steel) 13'' long by 5/8'' diameter, with a 'monkey' which slid up and down the stick of silver steel with a 'rocking' base which was finely adjusted by a threaded set screw. The scriber was made, once again from silver steel ¼'' in diameter and once again 13'' long. We had to file, and then highly polish a taper on each end in a collet lathe running at high speed, and then harden and 'temper' the two tapered ends of the silver steel. To harden high carbon steel, one heats the taper up to 'cherry' red and then quickly plunges the taper into a bucket of cold water. Then the scriber has to be polished again, and then tempered to a 'light straw; colour over a Bunsen burner flame, and then, once again plunged into the bucket of cold water. This 'sets' the steel to the required hardness forever. This tempering is done to 'let the steel down' a little because, if left in its 'glass hard' state after hardening the scriber would be brittle and would just chip off, the colours which show up when heated vary as the temperature of the steel being heat treated rises. Different applications, or jobs have to be tempered to different temperatures depending on what they were going to be used for. For example, a chisel needs to be 'let down' further than a scriber because the 'shock loads' when being struck by a hammer, so the tempering colour at the tip of the chisel is different from that on a scriber, the colour corresponding to the level of hardness plus durability. In a chisels case the colour would be dark blue. I loved this part of the job. It was fascinating, care being needed during the whole process. The tempering colours are similar to that of a rainbow, except that the colours are different. One can get books out of the library about heat treatments of materials-fascinating. The scribing block itself was made of 'mild' steel which cannot be hardened and tempered because it doesn't contain carbon, the block was about 5'' long, by about 3 ½'' wide by about 1 5/8th thick. This block had to be 'milled' on a milling machine to shape, then surface ground on a surface grinding machine which gives the base of the block a beautiful flat, shining surface. The surface grinding was done last after the block was filed up to erase the milling machines comparatively rough finish, then polished with coarse and fine emery cloth torn into strips and held along the length of a file. Then the block was 'blued' in the special steel oven over a gas ring as described earlier, then surface ground. At this time my mother had a breakdown following a hysterectomy, and Bert, the tool storeman, who was a horrible man who used to make one repeat one's request for say feeler gauges or whatever, would shout at one 'ow much ooo' (How much who) asked me one morning 'is that right your mother is in Bexley hospital?' I was surprised at this and said 'yes, she's in Ferndale ward.' Bert said 'my wife's in there too. She knows your mum.' I was gob-smacked at this. I had something in common with Bert- perhaps he will be a little more lenient with me now. He wasn't. He had a handlebar moustache partially hiding a terrible yellow scar which was caused by molten steel splashing on his face. His upper lip was swollen from this scar. I dreaded going to the tool store. One morning in the spring of 1961, I had just started work and it was a lovely warm morning, so I went out to the locker room and was pulling my jumper off when Mr Stephens called out to me as he was passing by 'what- you running hot son?' I blushed and grinned and just said one word, which was all I could think of. 'Yes'. I was lost for words, I had so much respect and administration for him. Another time he told me that he lived in Belvedere and said to me 'I expect you're one of the Belvedere boys.' I said, 'Yes I am'. He smiled and said, 'So was I' He had black shiny wavy hair always trimmed at the back, and black and silver side burns. I had become very good friends with Geoff Worham, the owner of the Velocette Venom I wrote about earlier on and he took me on the pillion to Maidstone County Hall where I got my first provisional motorcycle license 'over the counter'. We were doing 105mph down Wrotham Hill, and got from Mottingham, where he lived, to Maidstone in 26 mins, a distance of 26 miles! A mile a minute. We overtook a big American car in third gear doing 90mph, and we waved him. Geoff was mad but a skilled rider who said I was the best pillion passenger he had ever had, he said I was just heavy enough to keep the back wheel down! We were going through bends heeled over at 45 degrees, our boots and foot rest rubbers were grazing the ground, and on right handers the silencer (fish tail) sending up showers of sparks! I got my first bike in April 1961, a Triumph Tiger Cub, a single cylinder 199cc bike. The price was £99 cash, or £131 total hire purchase price. I brought it on hire purchase. It was delivered from Catford, South East London, to our door on the back of a small lorry. Barry Hazelwood, who lived near us, gave me an ex-world war 2 dispatch riders helmet, which made me look so foolish that I wouldn't wear it. I was young and very self-conscious. Barry and his older brother Ronnie Hazelwood, used to come over to our back scullery and serenade my mum with popular songs of the day, and they were dammed good. I was green with envy. They were both apprentices in Fraser and Chalmers Engineering works, making steam turbines for power stations and both went to Australia when they finished their 'time' at Frasers, and worked for Rio Tinto Zinc for a couple of years, and then came back to England. They were lovely men who both got married and had families. Barry was 3 years older than me and Ronnie 5 years older. Barry told me how their bodies got covered in red dust when working for Rio Tinto Zinc, even though they tied string around legs of the boiler suits just below the knee. 'that dust got everywhere' said

Barry. Frasers was situated on Fraser road, Erith, about a mile and a half from Belvedere, Upper Belvedere was more up market, where some fine big houses were, and where our Doctor, Doctor Malone, lived. I will always remember a photograph of him and his wife sitting out in the sun on a hotel balcony, somewhere in the Caribbean. They had cocktails on the table they were sitting at. He was a character, he was, if ever there was one. When my mum was having her first breakdown and lying-in bed as she was afraid of people, and life in general. Dr Malone came to see her, and he told her a joke which went like this 'This lady drank a bottle of Harpic and went clean round the bend.' My mum just couldn't see the funny side of the joke, or anything else at that time. The photograph of Dr F L G Malone (Francis Laurence Graham) and his wife was in the Kentish Times.

Back to the grind. The last job we did was to make set squares or try squares, large and small, under Mr Jack Connors. We had to cut right angle pieces of steel plate with a hacksaw, the large one being 8" high by 1 3/8" wide, one tenth of an inch thick, and the base of the try square was 4 ½" long by once again, 1 3/8" wide. The overall thickness of the base was ¾" made up of 2 pieces of steel riveted to the base, one each side of the length of a ¾ inch thick base of the try square. The 'sandwich' of the pieces of steel had to be clamped together, in the exact position, and drilled right through with 5 1/8" diameter holes, then countersunk, and the rivets, with the head of the rivets already the correct shape to fit the countersunk holes, and cut, with a hacksaw, to the correct length. Then one had to put a punch into the vice, and grip it tightly, and rivet by hammering the plain end of the rivet so that it filled the countersink then the round part of the hammered in rivet was filed flat and then polished with strips of coarse then fine emery cloth, held along the length of the file, so that not a trace of the rivet could be seen. The try square had to be checked for squareness with strips of cigarette paper, (3 of them) slipped between the master square and your square. If one strip of cigarette paper wasn't gripping between the two squares, you had to go away to your vice and holding the square lightly file just a wee bit off and take it back again, and again, until you got it right. The small square was done in the same way. We also made two centre punches and two scribers, all hardened and tempered out of silver steel. That was all our tools made. They were minutely checked over by Mr Thompson, our Foreman. He was very ill with his lungs, and on the way out. He was a miserable old bastard who never smiled. We were marked out of 100 for our tools and two boys tied with 85. Mr Stevens took me aside and said, 'How many marks do you think you've got, lad?' I said, 'About 70?' He then said, 'You have got 73, alright?' He had very kindly broken the news to me gently. The reason my mark wasn't so high as the other boys, was because I ran 2 months over the 7 months allowed to make the tools. I was happy with the decision. It was very fair. I did my utmost to make as good a kit of tools as possible and wasn't worried about the time it took. The day came when I was given a special pass to get my tools past the MOD policeman on the main gate and take them home to keep forever, and I felt very proud of myself when showing my mother and father that evening. My mum couldn't believe that I'd made them myself, and my dad was very proud of me. So was my nan and granddad when they saw my tools. One incident I must relate to you that was particularly cruel and shows what some people would do for a laugh. Poor Ken Wall, one of the apprentices, was tied with rope to two lamp fixtures on the fitters bench he was working on, his arms outstretched like Jesus, when he was nailed to the cross. He was left there all the dinner hour. Mr Staveley discovered him when he came back from eating his sandwiches, and told all that whoever did it would be sacked if they were found out. He used the word 'crucified' to describe this cruel act that they had perpetrated on this innocent young man, who would never ever answer back to anyone, and was harmless. Mr Staveley was an east end Jew, hence the word 'crucified'. The time came in June 1961, when we were told we would be going for the next few years of our apprenticeships. Peter Happy went to the light gun factory (D95), so did Geoff Worham and Howard 'Dusty' Jeanes, and Tony Porcher, and a few others, including me. I was well pleased to be going with two of my best mates- Peter Happy and Geoff Worham. The light gun factory made 105- and 120-millimetre tank guns, the 120mm tank gun being 21 feet long, 7 yards! 81mm mortars were also made in the light gun, and 'Wombat' anti-tank guns, and 25 pounder field guns. The workshop was the length and width a football pitch! It was divided into 7 'bays', And I was put down 7 bay on the fitting section, under Les Perryman, 6'3" tall, heavy-boned, but spare, with enormous hands. He was over 60, not far off retirement, and was brilliant. I called him 'Sir' for about 3 months before I dare call him Les! He said I should make bearing Scrapers, one large and one small, and flat scrapers, one large and one small. The bearing scrapers were made from old half round files, and the flat scrapers from old flat files. The old files had to be annealed (softened) by heating them up on a gas fired small forge, 'til they were red hot, and then allowed to cool down as slowly as possible, the opposite of the hardening process, where the old file would be heated up, and then plunged into a bucket of cold water. I also made a set of screwdrivers out of silver steel and I did the hardening and the tempering myself. I forgot to mention that while I was in the training shop I started for a little while to use my motorcycle for work, and one evening I couldn't get it started, and Mr Alec Stevens came out of his office and gave me a push to bump start it. He took quite a shine to me, I'm very proud to say.

Back to the Light Gun Factory. In February 1962, Les asked me would I like to come down the abbey wood end to the proof butts, as a tank gun (120mm) was going to be tested. The gas tight seal in the breech of the gun was made by the OBTURATOR SLEEVE and OBTURATOR INSERT. One fitted into the Breech End of the Gun Barrel. Both were surface ground and then 'lapped' flat, perfectly flat, with lapping paste. The obturators were made to a clever design so that the more pressure that was exerted on the seal, the tighter it got. Les had had to stone, with a carborundum stone about ½'' square and 6'' long, a small groove across the face of the lapped flat obturator, 30 thou deep by about 050'' (50 thou) wide, to see how many rounds could be fired before the Breech was ruined. Les had been issued with 2 duffle coats and gave 1 to me to wear. The weather that morning was crystal clear but with a hard frost. When I put the duffle coat on, it was dragging along the ground, as I was so little and Les was so large! We were driven down to the Proof Butts in an army staff car. The journey took about 10 minutes and we parked outside the Proof Butts, so that the car was out of danger. What a sight the proof butts where. They were made of bricks, 2 feet thick, each one about 30 feet wide by almost 20 feet high, and about 30feet from front to back, the back being a brick wall 2 feet thick, and half full of sand. The Proof Butts stretched away about 150 yards, about 15 of them numbered in faded white paint. To the right, about 30 yards from us were special railway wagons, made to hold a 16'',60-foot-long Battleship Gun. The rails ran back and then up a curved slope, with buffers at the top. The big guns, when fired, recoiled along the track, up the slope and back again, the 16'' shell burying itself in the sand, when it had to be dug out by 'sand rats', a name the men who dug them out were saddled with. Our gun, at 120mm, or 4.8 inches, as near as dammit, was mounted solidly and, on 2 sides had concreate blocks. 4 feet long by 18 inches square, with a steel plate 8 feet high by about 8 feet wide, with a hole top centre where a crane, a mobile cane, slid it across to seal the Breech of the gun off, just in case the Breech blew to pieces. The 120mm shells had a high-speed spin put on them as they flew through the air by P.T.F.E. (Nylon) driving bands which where rammed into the sharp start of the riffing (RIFLING) by one of the fitters, then a 'BAG CHARGE' of high explosives was pushed in behind the shell. Then the breech slammed shut and the gun was ready to fire. The bag charge was made of canvas, 6'' in diameter by about 18'' long and canvas ends sewn on. The spinning shell would be straight and true because of the spin, otherwise it would start tumbling end over end and go all over the place, missing the target altogether. The gun loaded, everyone retired underground in a concrete bunker down a set of concrete stairs except - guess who? Little dare devil me! A siren sounded and a red flag was raised and the gun went off with an ear-splitting BANG. All the air in my lungs was knocked out of me by the pressure wave of the blast, and then 7 or 8 beautiful smoke rings issued from the muzzle of the gun, a beautiful blue in colour, one after another, where they expanded to about 3 or 4 feet in diameter where they just dissipated in to thin air about 8 yards from the muzzle of the gun, WHAT A BEAUTIFUL SIGHT! The Breech only withstood 3 rounds and the gun was scrap. Les' little groove was widened to a 1'' and a ½'' as if it were cut open by a welding torch. No one noticed, thank god, that I hadn't gone down the bunker, so I was jubilant! My ears were ringing for about 10 minutes after the gun went off. The 'all clear' was sounded and the flag was lowered, and we were driven 'home' to the light gun, for lunch or dinner, whichever you prefer. I was then going to the BOX REPAIR canteen, excellent food. I will tell you about the light gun mess now. First of all, let me say that there were 5 canteens in the arsenal, the flag staff, up near central office, the Box Repair, the Tailor shop, and 2 others, whose names escape me at this distance in time. The Light Gun Mess was a magical place. As soon as we found it, which wasn't easy, on entering there was a strong smell of beer! Yes BEER. It also served as a canteen for the men who worked in the forges, years ago, the men who worked in the forges were given an allowance for 8 pints of beer a day as it was such an arduous and thirsty job, them men losing pints of sweat every day. Peter Happy took me over there to show me it. We had a good look round and then went back to the Light Gun, negotiating a maze of smaller workshops on the way. The Light Gun mess had a well-stocked bar, with spirits, whisky, rum, gin etc. Let's go 'up the park' and climb the huge Copper Beech tree along the 'dirt pitch' so called because nothing grew under the Copper

Beech, it was all leaf, mould, and earth. The first time we climbed it I was 14 years old. The first branch was about 12 feet above the ground, and a ladder was necessary, but once up on the first bough it was fairly easy going right up to the top and took about 10 minutes or so. The view from up there was fantastic, the canopies of all the other trees were perfectly hemispherical, like a football, and one felt that they could walk over the tops of all these beautiful treetops. We only found out when we got to the top that there was another Copper Beech about 40 yards up the valley, we never spotted it from down on ground level. Right up the top, about 70- feet up were some very old initials grown fat by the expansion of the boughs, stretching the bark. The initials read – H.G. 1912. How about that! In the direction north you could see over Picardy school roofs, and right down to the Thames, to Belvedere Power Station and directly across the River Ford of Dagenham, and Cross Ness Sewage works, also known as the Southern Outfall. At this time (1959), they were still pouring raw sewage into the Thames when the tide was going out and when the tide was out exposing the mudflats, on a hot summers day with the wind blowing from North-to-North East, the smell was overpowering. They now use 'Bovril Boats' full of sewage which they take out to the North Sea, where they dump it out of huge, hinged 'doors' which run along each side of the keel. They are opened out at Sea, and a boat load of sewage is dumped and sinks down to the bottom. Cross Ness Sewage works on the South Bank of the Thames about a quarter of a mile from Belvedere Power Station on our side of the Thames. The river is much cleaner now, and some years ago a large Salmon was found trapped in the intake pipe for cold water to be used in the condensers in the power station. I will tell you all about condensers, and Power stations, as I was working in the arsenal's own Power station during the last year of my apprenticeship. That will come later if you'll bear with me! Our hands were black with soot from climbing up the copper beech, this soot was from the industry over the other side of the railway line. I did that climb up the copper beech again for old times' sake, when I was in my late 30's. I pulled the ladder up into the tree, so that no one could steal it. I was very nostalgic for those times when I was a teenager, more of that anon. Back down 7 Bay in the Light Gun. I got to know the men well, especially Georgie Pine, a man of about 45 years old and very fit from fitting the Breech Blocks into the Breech Rings of the 120mm tank guns and playing cricket for Bexleyheath. The man who slotted out the aperture in the Breech Rings on a huge Slotting machine would leave just a few 'thou' for Georgie Pine to file them out to a beautiful fit with the Breech Blocks, which had to slide up and down the Breech ring closing and opening the Breech for a gunner in the turret of the tank to reload a new shell and bag charge, ready to fire when in Battle. After firing, when the Breech was opened there was nothing left of the Bag charge, it was atomised. At this time, I was asked to make a Duralumin (aluminium alloy) Pulley for an electric motor. I made the pulley and half a dozen men gathered round, some I'm sure, expecting my pully to run out of true. It ran dead true and I was immediately in Georgie Pines good books, as there was nothing he regarded more highly than a good workman, and I was very good at my job, but still learning at the time. When George was filing out the aperture in the Beech Ring for the fitting of the Breech Block, if you got near him you could smell the sweat in his armpits, it was hard graft.

He told me that before and during the war he used to get on a trolly laying on his front and he would be pulled up inside the 16'' guns to check the rifling, and if there were any tears in the rifling, he had to clean them up with a file. A powerful, electric light would be shone down the barrel so that he could see what he was doing. I also met Sam Monk at this time. He was enormously powerful, all bone and muscle and known as the 'mad monk'. He used to lift the Breech Blocks off of a small but extremely strong trolly on to the 'table' of his large surface grinding machine. They weighed 1 1/2th hundredweight (EACH!) He made me laugh one day- he lifted a Breech Block off the trolley onto the 'table' of the machine, and then pretending to push an old rupture in his groin, back in. His mood could change though. One day you could talk to him, another day you couldn't. He was up and down like a yo-yo and could be dangerous when roused. I had to be very circumspect. In the light gun at that time were 2 nice fellows, who were engravers working on a variety of engraving machines, one of them was about 35, and the other about 48-50, and he used to be a hairdresser and had a nice little clandestine business going on out in the 'nutty grinders' workshop, cutting men's hair for half as much as they were charged outside. He used to do mine for nothing – 'gratis', and one time he had just finished my hair, and he said to me, 'Now you watch out for them big soldiers.' It took me about 10 seconds to cotton on and then I blushed furiously, like a little girl! They were both nice blokes, who had a nice, clean job engraving warning notices which were screwed into position on the various guns. 'The nutty grinders' Were working on surface and rotary grinding machines to very fine limits and had loudspeakers rigged up in the workshop

41

playing beautiful music all day. It was delightful. Their workshop was about 20 yards long by about 10 yards wide, very small compared to the Light Gun proper. When I was about 11 years old and my next brother down was 9, my Dad took us up to the Woolwich stadium to watch a game of Hurling. Dublin were playing Wexford, and Dad said, 'Keep on shouting 'Up Dublin' We duly kept shouting 'Up Dublin' and by that evening we had both shouted ourselves hoarse! We could hardly speak! I remember 3 men went into a tackle, there was an ear splitting 'CRACK' and the business end of 3 Hurley's went cartwheeling up 60 feet into the air- what a game, but the score I just can't remember! Hurling is the fastest game in the world. Back in the arsenal a man by the name of Bob Plum said to me one morning 'Come on over to the forges they will be forging a tank gun at 10 o'clock' Bob Plum was about medium height, always wore a sweat stained trilby and a brown smock, undone. He was built like a battleship, his trousers at half mast, and the sleeves of his smock rolled up halfway between his wrists and his elbows revealing thick, hairy forearms and muscular hands like dinner plates. He never seemed to have a job to do, he was on a roving commission! I had never been in the forges before and followed Bob. We went into this building and what a sight greeted my startled gaze. There was a 1,500-ton steam press, the ram going up and down, pressing this lump of bright yellow steel, which was being turned round and round by an overhead gantry crane running on tracks 20 feet apart running the length of the forge, the steel being suspended and turned by a gigantic 'bicycle chain', each link as big as your head, and the heavy lump of steel counterbalanced by a log of wood bark taken off, clamped to the Breech end of the forging by two clamps made of steel, like a gigantic clothes peg and slotted on tightly by 4 long clamping bolts and 1 ½'' diameters by 18 inches long, with nuts and washers. This 'log' was about 12 feet long with a large 'car tyre' of solid steel looped over it. 3 men were also 'draped' across this log on their stomach muscles as the press gradually drew out the long slow tapered muzzle end of the barrel. The heat from this steel was intense, one had to stand back not only from the heat but for safety's sake as well. The skill of the man operating the press was a sight to behold. He was controlling the ram by a 'T bar' a length of steel about 4 ½ feet long with a 'T bar' across the top. The man had to push the 'T Bar' away to make the ram come down onto the glowing yellow steel and pull it back to make the ram rise up off the forging. Gradually the barrel grew in the length as the diameter was reduced and he had to work fast as the forging was gradually losing heat. At last, a long steel tape rule was laid along the length, overall, of the barrel and another man brought an axe like, long handled tool and the barrel was sliced off to length, like a knife through cheese. Every time the ram was raised there was a loud hiss of steam as the pressure was released. What a sight for a 16-year-old! I went back the following morning on my own just as 2 bricklayers were sealing another large billet of steel into the furnace, which was coal fired. They were using firebricks and mortar. The billet was almost completely enveloped in the furnace, just about 6'' showing. Another man was shovelling coal into an aperture about 2 feet square feeding the white-hot inside of the furnace, throwing the coal about 10 feet through the air straight into the coal-hole. I had seen enough and went back into the Light Gun. One week Alec and I went cycling down along the River Bank and Alec spotted a hand cranked siren bolted to a stout wooden gate. He said he was going to go home to get some spanners to dismantle the siren and carry it home on his bicycle carrier. We duly dismantled the siren and rode home. It was quite heavy but we got home and carried the siren up into the park, up the top of the 'dell' and started to wind the handle, a loud wailing noise just like a second world war siren began to sound from the siren, which must have terrorised some poor folks, and a couple of minutes later a young woman with a howling baby in her arms started shouting at us to stop it. We stopped immediately and never did it again. What became of that siren God only knows, we were little buggers, Alec and I. Alec also used to make pipe bombs from old bicycle frames cut into 10'' lengths. He would hammer one end tightly down flat like the end of a tube of tooth paste, fill up the tube with a mixture of white powdered weed killer and sugar, buy a length of fuse wire, insert one end of the wire into the weed killer and sugar, hammer the end down tightly, cut the fuse wire to length (about 6 feet) then he tied the pipe bomb to the top of a reinforced concrete fence post, lit the fuse wire and we ran for cover. The bomb went off with a terrific bang and we came out of hiding to see the result. The top 3 feet of concrete was completely blown away and the 3 steel rods which reinforced the concrete were bent and twisted. The force of the blast was terrific, he used to get up to all sorts of tricks down in his fathers shed. Another time he made a leather sling with a pouch for the projectile (up to half a house brick) with two leather sling straps. One night when the street lights were on, he stood under a light with a large stone in the pouch, wound the sling round and round and let go of one leather strap and somehow smashed the street light to pieces.

We ran like hell into the park and hid for half an hour 'til it was all clear. The street light was one of the new-fangled orange lights, very stoutly made, but the whole lot came down in pieces. We were a right pair, but I acted like a brake on him, if it hadn't been for me, he would have ended up in jail. After my year with Les Perryman fitting, I was put with a man called Wally Rickets for 2 years turning. He was a swine and I was so scared of him but he had a reputation for being one of the best turners in the workshop. One job I did was two copper discs with a 1" hole through the centre. I bored out the holes with boring tool as accurately as I could with the spring calipers and a 1" micrometre. Wally got out a 1" plain plug gauge out of the tool store to check them with. They were both bang on size, and he said to me 'I think you're going to be even better than I am' then he realised what he'd said and said, 'Not that that's that good'. Back to Seamen's home and Prince. The Seamen's home was a huge, very old stately home called Belvedere House, and owned by Lord Eardley. There is a pub at the top of Heron Hill called the Eardley arms, it was brought by the Royal Alfred Merchant Seamen's Society, for old and infirm ex-merchant seamen, and had about 20 acres of virgin woodland, and hills and dales. There was also an almost vertical, hard packed sandy cliff about 20 feet high by about 25 yards wide. There was a freshly dug fox hole about halfway up the cliff, and one weekend a few of us climbed up to the hole with prince, our dog. He was in his prime and very courageous. Straight away, before I could stop him, he dived down the fox hole and about 10 seconds later, he came out backwards with a little fox cub by the scruff of its neck! He dropped it and was looking down very quizzically at it. The little thing looked around, and then scampered back down the hole. Prince went back after it. I just managed to grab the end of his tail and dragged him back out! I took him by the collar and took him away from the hole and took him home, as I didn't want him getting stuck down the hole. Another time we were climbing a tree which had fallen and propped itself against another big tree at an angle of about 45 degrees. I was climbing up the fallen tree and blow me if Prince didn't climb up behind me! I thought 'God, how is he going to get back down?' I got hold of his collar and slowly climbed down backwards down the sloping tree hoping he wouldn't slip off as we were about 20 feet up. Once again, having got him down, I had to take him home. He had bags of stamina and would chase foxes for hours. One weekend we were in the Seamen's home grounds, and a fox jumped up onto this big fallen log, ran along it, jumped off, darted across this clearing, and disappeared into brambles. A full minute later, there was a crashing in the undergrowth and prince appearing jumped up onto the fallen tree, nose down following the scent of this fox. He jumped off the tree exactly where the fox had sprinted across the clearing and went crashing into the brambles in hot pursuit! He was a fantastic dog altogether. When I was 19 years old, I brought an old 1939 350 cc Velocette. The valve gear was making a clattering sound, and I decided to strip the engine right down and find out what the trouble was and fix it. I found that the exhaust valve was partly sticking in its guide, caused the noise, I took both the exhaust valve and inlet valve into work, polished the carbon off the exhaust valve and also polished the inlet valve. I then asked one of the grinders would he grind the valve seats. He did this small job for nothing, I made a new exhaust valve guide out of my nodular cast iron, which

Wally Ricketts told me was the right stuff to use. I also found that the timing side main bearing had worked loose on the timing side main shaft. I smuggled the flywheels into the arsenal, took them apart, fitted 0004'' tenths of a thou oversize rollers to the Big End and fixed the timing side main shaft where the ball race had worked loose. I brought 2 new roller races, made by Hoffmann, arguably the best bearing manufacturer in the world, fitted them onto the drive side and timing side main shafts, put the flywheels back together, got the whole lot running dead true, within 1 thousandth of an inch, smuggled the valves and flywheels out of the arsenal, put the whole lot together at home, fitted the engine back into the frame, and to my immense satisfaction, it cured the problem, I was getting to know my job inside out. I had an old workshop manual which came with the bike, and followed it carefully step by step. I then brought Vincent Pattern straight handlebars for it, and it looked a treat. It had Webb girder forks, (the best) and rigid frame, meaning no rear suspension, and on a number of occasions I was knocked nearly sick when out riding and didn't see a hollow in the road ahead and dropped down into it to be bounced back up again when coming out of the far side. I had it two years when I wrecked the girder forks by running into the back bumper of a minivan which had stopped suddenly about 6 or 7 yards in front of me at the traffic lights at the bottom of shooters hill. The forks were bent into a zig zag and I nearly wept. With an elderly ladies' permission, I dropped it into her front garden, walked 5 miles home, got a hacksaw, went back, and cut the aluminium front mud guard free from the tyre and made it home. I sold it to a friend for £5. The Light Gun foreman's name was Mr Kettle Williams and he appeared on BBC television one weekend on the programme 'Come Dancing'. He was formation dancing with about a dozen other couples. David Jacobs was the anchor man on the program. Mr Kettle Williams stuck out like a sore thumb as he didn't have any hair on his head, or anywhere else on his body because of some illness he had had. Just about everyone in the world watched it! They were jolly good. Kettle Williams was built like a dancer, perfectly proportioned and always smart and well turned out. He was in his fifties at that time. Christmas at the light gun Factory was bloody marvellous. The last day at work before the holiday no work was done. Trestle tables were set up down 3 Bay about 20 yards long with shining white table cloths and laden with sandwiches, sausage rolls and cake. In the afternoon crates of beer and spirits would be arranged on the tables and the eating and drinking began. Peter Happy said 'We need to line our stomachs with food Kev, let's go to the canteen and have dinner.' We lined our stomachs with stew and 3 lots of afters. We went back to the Light Gun and had a good drink- just beer, no spirits. At 4 o'clock men started to go home. None of us apprentices had ridden our bikes into work so we could have a good drink. I started out on my way home and the fresh air made me drunk as a Lord! How I got home I don't know, all I know is that I got home and went straight up the stairs, went in my mother and father's bedroom, and threw myself on the bed. I laid on my back and looked up at the ceiling. First it started spinning round one way, then it stopped and started spinning round the other way. I turned onto my side and was sick as a dog! All that food and drink made a 'halo' round my head, and I just lay there, a splitting headache coming on. My mum discovered me ½ an hour later, but she never complained or moaned at me, she just told me to go and get in the bath. I have never felt so ill in all my life and learned my lesson. I have never been in such a state since or anywhere near it. The names of the apprentices that I can remember are Maurice Styles, Mick Happy, Peters older brother Geoff Worham, Peter Happy, Barry Rundle, Ron Phasey, Tom Oldfield, Dick Cove, Keith McAvoy (Mac), Keith Bedwell, Howard Jeanes (Dusty), Paddy Farrell, Ken Wall, Lefty Wright, Peter Kemp (Jumbo), and Uncle Tom Cobley and all! Paddy Farrell was over from Ireland to do his apprenticeship, he was 6'6 tall and gangly, with thick, pebble lens glasses and he stunk, so much that no one could get near him. He was warned about this 3 times in writing, but wouldn't wash, so he was sacked. Barry Rundle was 6'3 and 19 stone, a huge young man, and Ron Phasey was 6'5 and 17 stone at the age of 17. Peter Kemp was 5'10 and 16 stone, hence the nickname 'Jumbo', and owned a 350cc BSA Gold Star. There was a mile long straight down the Abbey Wood end with a fast bend at the end near the 5th gate, and this straight was called the Berber or Ber Ber road after a North African tribe called the Berbers or Ber Bers. Peter was, when he got astride his bike, a madman, and he came off one day when going into this bend at the end of the road doing 70mph, but got away with grazed knees and elbows, the bike sustained a small tear at the back of the dual seat and the top of the speedo and rev counter was grazed. He was very lucky, I forgot to mention Tony Porcher who was about 5'3 tall, but very stocky, and one day we were playing football outside the Light Gun, when a loose ball came our way. We both sprinted, neck and neck for the ball and I timed a shoulder charge perfectly, and he went sprawling in the dust when I got possession of the ball, a cheer went up from the others. Tony didn't like it one bit. Another time we were messing about with this fire hydrant, (they were all over the arsenal). Which stood about 2 feet high. These hydrants had 2 outlets for two hoses, with Brass stoppers on short chains, so that they wouldn't get lost. Big Barry Rundle booted both stoppers in tight and dared someone to open the valve, by a cast iron hand wheel on the top. The hydrants where painted red. Tony Porcher was standing about 5 feet from one of the stoppers. I took my courage in both hands, went forward, and spun the cast iron hand wheel wide open. The stopper on Tony's side burst out with a bang and he was soaked from, head to foot. Everyone was falling about laughing except tony! He forgave me and I lent him one of my khaki tank suits, like a boiler suit. He went up to the locker room, changed out of his soaking clothes and put the tank suit on. That evening he went home in the tank suit! I saw a sight that very few people have seen one day in the 'Shrinking pits' a red-hot gun barrel was being heat treated. It was lowered, red hot, into a deep vat of cold oil, God knows how deep and about 6 feet in diameter. It went in, breech end first, and the oil started bubbling. When there was about 5 feet of the muzzle end still to go a yellow flame came out of the bore of the gun and went up 6 feet into the air. By this time there was black smoke coming out of the surface of the oil which was bubbling quite fast when the surface of the oil caught fire. What a sight. 3 firemen were standing by the foam extinguishers which they sprayed with a loud hissing sound onto the surface of the oil extinguishing the flames within about 15 seconds. The barrel was lowered right down 6 feet under the surface and left all night to go cold in the oil. This process stiffened and toughened the barrel which was then finish turned and rifled.

While I was with Wally Rickets, I was asked one day would I scrape the aluminium 'A' frame to fit a rotary ground shaft. This meant going back over to 7 Bay to do the job. I was just about 20 years old. I said I would, and one of the charge hands showed me the job. I went to my toolbox and took my big bearing scraper out, blued the shaft with engineer's blue and lifted the shaft which was about 2ft 3 inches long and 2 ¼ inches in diameter and placed it in the 2 'bores' and gave the shaft another rub. Gradually the shaft sank into the 'bores' completely and I was satisfied. The chargehand said, 'That's fine lad, good job' it had taken about ½ an hour. I was glad when the time came to leave Wally Ricketts and move over to the gear cutting and broaching section right down the bottom of 1 Bay. I was introduced to this man of about 50 with a silver bristling moustache and silver hair, whose name was Jim somebody or other. He showed me a gear cutting machine in action and the complicated mathematics which goes into the design of such a machine. I was then given some broaching to do. This machine was about 10 feet long and hydraulically actuated. I had to broach several dozen actuating arms, which opened and closed the breech of the 120 mm tank gun. A spline had to be cut into a bore 2" in diameter and about 9" long. He gave me a very hard time regarding my religion, 'What do you need to go to confession for at your age' he said, quite testily. He was a militant atheist and gave me quite a 'battering'. I remain a catholic, in fact my religion has become stronger and deeper as I've got older. I am now nearly 75 years old and my belief is going from strength to strength. I was glad to leave him after a few months and my final stint of my apprenticeship was done in the Power Station, not Woolwich Power Station but the arsenals own Power Station. I was put with Denis Burroughs, who was round faced, about my height, and always wore a school boys cap, quartered blue and grey with a blue peak. He was about 60, still hale and hearty. He showed me round the turbine hall where 3 metropolitan Vickers turbine sets were working. There was a man of about 40 who was called the 'turbine driver' whose job it was to just check over once every half an hour or so, the 'turbine sets' to see that everything was in order. I shouted to him 'do you need any qualification to do your job' he just said 'No'. He didn't want to talk. I say I shouted at him because of the din. Denis showed me the generators which were driven by the turbine at high-speed generating electricity, and the enormous caron brushes rubbing against the copper windings of the rotors, and little sparks from the carbon brushes and copper windings. The windings were about 3'6 in diameter and about a foot wide. Denis was constantly taking snuff and then blowing his nose on a filthy handkerchief! We then went down to the floor beneath the 'turbine sets' where Denis showed me the condensers. These were about 5 feet in diameter and about 10 feet long. One of the 'turbine sets' was shut down while essential maintenance was carried out on the condensers. One end cover was unbolted and the trouble was there for all to see. There were 999 copper tubes passing along the length of the condensers and each and every one was clogged with used durex! A labourer wearing gloves had the unenviable task of pulling them out and dumping them into a large steel drum. Disgusting. Eventually the condenser was 'boxed up' and ready for action. These condensers were slung directly beneath the exhaust steam. Cold river water was pumped through all 999 pipes where the still hot steam, which was super-heated before being 'blown' through the turbines and had cooled to boiling point passed through the maze of pipes turning to pure water- condensed like rain water, and pumped round to the boiler house where the water was boiled again, and then super-heated for use in the turbines. Peter Happy, being a year older than me, left the arsenal and joined the R.F.A (Royal Fleet Auxiliary) as an engine room artificer. Just before he left, he came in to work one day, driving his father's Austin Westminster, a beautiful black and dark green two-tone colour. We had a grand tour around the arsenal, and then shook hands and I saw him once more about 1 month after I'd finished my time, when he was home on leave. He was showing off his new 3-piece tailor made suit which he got made in Hong Kong for £5. He came to our house in Belvedere to see how I was getting on. I never saw or heard from him again. I sometimes wonder is he a grandfather now, or even, maybe, a great grandfather. Or maybe, he remained a single man, who knows? I used to borrow our foreman's bicycle- a government issue blue bike, to cycle down the abbey wood end to do a bit of sunbathing and get away from it all. One day he wanted to use the bike in dinner hour and of course, I'd 'borrowed' it! He gave me a good telling off when I got back, but I did exactly the same the following day, the weather being lovely, and I got away with it. Foolhardy? Yes, extremely. One day I cycled down the footpath alongside the canal, where battle ship guns were towed down to the lock gates, giving access to the Thames. There was a 250-ton crane which lifted the guns onto a barge which was towed by a tugboat to the shipyard up river where they would be mounted in a turret on a Battleship ready for action. My father used to maintain that 250-ton crane. I cycled past an auburn-haired woman, sitting on the concrete side of the canal, eating jam sandwiches. I could see right up the underside of her thighs, a highly erotic sight to a sex starved catholic lad! As I went by, I called out, 'Can I have a bit?' She watched me go by, smiling at me. I was wearing a white short sleeved t shirt and tight blue jeans. I cycled on down to the lock gates, turned around and cycled back again. I pulled up by her, making sure I still had a clear view of her lovely plump thighs. She had one leg over the other- my God, what a sight. She asked me how I maintained my figure. I said, 'my job keeps me fit.' She asked me where did I work. I was getting more and more excited and it showed! She didn't know the arsenal had its own Power Station. I cycled back with her when it was time to go and asked her would she be back there again the following day but she wouldn't commit herself. Next day the weather had changed completely, being overcast and windy- alas, she wasn't there. She must have been 30 years older than me and, possibly a grandmother. End of story! On the 'coaling plant' in the Power Station, was a man by the name of Fred Phoebe, and he rode a Lambretta scooter. He was built like a tank and lived in Bethnal Green. He was a boxing fan and used to go to watch fights live in Bethnal Green. One day he asked me would I like to meet his sister, who, like Fred, wasn't married. I said yes, and a few evenings later we rode on Fred's scooter to his and his sisters flat. I had already told Fred, who's sister had told him to ask what I liked for dinner, and I said 'Plaice and chips' she went to Billingsgate fish market and brought fresh plaice especially for me. She kept the flat spotless, and I liked her very much. The plaice and chips were delicious, and I thanked her and Fred proceeded to drive me all the way home. His back brake started to 'bind' halfway home, the heat in the brake steadily increasing until we were virtually brought to a standstill, smoke issuing from the break. Fred was terribly worried about me getting home, but as we were in Woolwich, I assured him I could get the train home, which I did. Fred was about 50 years old, and his sister around the same age. I saw Mick Happy carry out his starting drill one evening as we were all going home. He had acquired an old Jowett horizontally apposed flat twin van which was a bugger to start. He always carried a gallon can of petrol in the van, and what he did was to unscrew the 2 sparking plugs, take the petrol cap off the can, fill the cap with petrol and pour the cap full of petrol down the sparking plug hole of both cylinders, screw in the plugs, put the sparking plug caps back on and, hey presto, with the starting handle start it up. It was the only way to get it started! I wouldn't have believed it unless I had seen it with my own eyes. Fred Phoebe brought a nice boat of about 12 feet in length with a lovely little marine twin cylinder engine amidships, with a seat at the stern with a tiller to steer it with. There was another seat in the bow. He invited me to his father's house in Broxbourne in Hertfordshire. One of the labourers in the Power Station told me after I had agreed to go along for the ride that he wouldn't trust Fred with his cat! I had only a few days of my apprenticeship to complete so I went anyway. We had to climb down slippery concrete steps to get to the boat and we had a lighterman take us across the River Thames and into this lock. The lighterman was as agile as a monkey and shinned up the lock gate while we held the boat steady, and about a minute later the lock gate began to swing open letting us into the lock. The Lighterman then shut the lock gate and opened the sluice on the other gate letting the water level rise 'til he could open the second gate, and

Fred started the little diesel engine and away we went along the river Lea through Poplar and Bow, eventually leaving London behind and getting into deepest Hertfordshire. The river meandered to left and right passing some big half-timbered mansions on the way. The countryside was lovely, it being midsummer the weather was warm and dry, all the trees in full leaf. Fred said, 'Come and have a go at steering her Kev' and so I steered her the rest of the way to Broxbourne. It was dark by the time we arrived, and we tied the boat to his father's jetty, stopped the engine, and disembarked. Fred introduced me to his father who lived in a timber house with 2 or 3 outhouses, one of which I slept in. After a nightcap of tea with a drink of rum in it I went and got into bed. I hardly slept a wink, just dozed, until Fred knocked on the door and opened it. I was sitting on the bed cross legged with my underpants and a shirt on. Fred said, 'Look at you – a little hairy – Jack!' Then we went and had a fried egg on toast with his elderly father. Fred's mother was dead. The egg came from his father's own chickens- free range. Lovely they were with orange yolks. Fred didn't try any 'funny business' and drove me back home all the way to Belvedere on his Lambretta. A few days later I had to surrender my gate pass, was reminded of the official secrets act 1911, forbidding me to talk about the job for thirty years, I was handed a slip of paper authorising me to leave, and that was the end of my hardworking, sometimes a good laugh-apprenticeship. It is something whose memory I treasure to this day.

Woolwich is the 'Home' of the Royal Artillery, the Barracks being up on Woolwich Common, and the Parade Ground was, and maybe still is, the biggest in the world. It is about ¼ mile long by almost 100 yards wide! I have walked by there a number of times but have never seen the soldiers on parade. My mum and dad were married in Saint Peter's Church, Woolwich, the Catholic Church up new road opposite the Catholic Club, where we used to go with Dad, me and my brother Tony that is, where my dad would have a pint and Tony and I would have a lemonade and crisps, and go and punch the punch bag, which was used by St Peters Boxing Club, the best boxers for miles around, coming from the church and the club. We skinned our knuckles on the big punch bag, which was dangling from ceiling, and covered in coarse canvas. I can remember vaguely, my Mum and Dad dancing in the dance Hall to a live, resident band, the drummer leaving his drums there all the week set up for the following week. This was around 1950.

Happy Days.

One of the men in the Light Gun Factory had a battered old Royal Enfield Motorcycle combination which he sold to us apprentices for £5. It was well and truly knackered. The spokes in the side car wheel were sticking out at all angles, only about 1/3 of them were any good, the hood on the double adult side car was flapping in the wind, but we all used to pile into it and on it, one time we had 8 of us on board and we used to ride all around the arsenal on it. One dinner hour I was driving it with apprentices festooned all over it when we ran out of petrol. We stopped right close to a mobile crane. In the boot of the side car was a length of rubber tube about 6 feet long. We thought we could siphon off some petrol from the tank of the mobile crane. Written in chalk on the tank was the following 'Petrol, Paraffin 50/50'. We were desperate so I took the cap of the petrol tank, and the cap off the Royal Enfield's tank to siphon some 'juice' off. I put one end of the tube into the mobile cranes tank and sucked for all I was worth on the other end of the tube. Nothing happened. I sucked again and got an oily mouthful of petrol/paraffin. Once started it kept spouting this foul brew so I stuck the end into the Royal Enfield's tank and filled our tank. Peter Happy removed the tube from the mobile cranes tank and kick started the motor cycle. It actually ran on half and half petrol paraffin! The bike had a very low compression ratio otherwise it wouldn't have started. Off we went cheering and shouting, absolutely jubilant. How about that! Just a word about the Heavy Gun Factory, Building D75. Big Battleship Guns were obsolete but the huge gantry cranes which run up and down the workshop on rails were supported by massive girders painted dark green and were all still there and could lift 250 tons. The huge lathes which used to turn the barrels were also still there. It had been renamed the 'Tank Shop', not water tanks but Centurion Tanks. I think I will call it a day now; I could go on and on! The main gate to the arsenal and the old forges are listed buildings. That's it. Adios!